CROC: LEGEND OF THE GOBBOS REMASTER GAME GUIDE

Table of Contents

1. INTRODUCTION TO CROC: LEGEND OF THE GOBBOS REMASTER

1.1 Overview of the Remaster

Croc: Legend of the Gobbos Remaster is a modernized version of the beloved 1997 3D platformer originally developed by Argonaut Games. This remaster brings back the classic adventure of Croc, the courageous little crocodile, as he embarks on a journey to rescue the Gobbos from the evil Baron Dante.

Key Features of the Remaster:

- Enhanced Graphics & Visuals
  The game now features high-definition textures, improved lighting, and smoother animations while maintaining the original charm and art style.
- Refined Controls & Gameplay Improvements
  The remaster updates Croc's movement, making jumps and combat feel more responsive, and adjusts the camera system for a more user-friendly experience.
- Remastered Soundtrack & Audio Enhancements
  The original soundtrack has been re-recorded with higher-quality instruments, and sound effects have been improved for better immersion.
- Additional Content & Secrets
  New unlockables, secret areas, and bonus levels have been added, giving both newcomers and veterans fresh challenges to explore.

- Multiple Difficulty Options
  The remaster includes different difficulty settings to accommodate both casual players and hardcore fans of the original game.

This remaster aims to bring the nostalgia of the classic *Croc: Legend of the Gobbos* to modern platforms while refining its gameplay for a new generation of players.

1.2 Key Differences from the Original

While *Croc: Legend of the Gobbos Remaster* stays true to the core gameplay of the 1997 classic, several improvements and changes have been made to modernize the experience. Here are the key differences between the remaster and the original game:

1. Graphical and Visual Upgrades

- The remaster features fully reworked HD textures, improved lighting, and updated character models.
- The environments have more detail, with enhanced water effects, better shadows, and smoother animations.
- Croc and the Gobbos have been redesigned with more expressive animations while keeping their classic look intact.

2. Improved Controls & Camera System

- The original tank-style movement has been replaced with a more fluid, modern control scheme, making jumps and platforming smoother.

- The camera system is now fully adjustable, eliminating the stiff and sometimes frustrating camera angles from the original.
- New movement options such as mid-air adjustments allow for more precise platforming.

3. Enhanced Audio & Soundtrack

- The entire soundtrack has been remastered with orchestral and high-quality sound arrangements.
- Sound effects, such as Croc's jumps, enemy sounds, and environmental audio, have been re-recorded for a richer experience.
- Voice clips and character expressions have been slightly expanded, giving Croc and the Gobbos more personality.

4. Additional Content & Gameplay Tweaks

- New unlockable levels and secret areas provide fresh challenges even for veteran players.
- Alternate skins and costumes for Croc can now be unlocked by collecting hidden items.
- More collectibles and expanded bonus stages add extra replayability.

5. Updated Difficulty and Quality of Life Improvements

The remaster introduces multiple difficulty settings, allowing players to choose between an easier mode for casual play or a harder mode for a classic challenge.

Save system improvements: The game now features auto-save and manual save options instead of relying on passwords or limited save points.

Checkpoints have been adjusted to be more forgiving without making the game too easy.

1.3 Storyline Recap

Croc: Legend of the Gobbos Remaster follows the adventure of Croc, a courageous young crocodile raised by the friendly and peaceful Gobbos. The game's story remains faithful to the original, with a few added cutscenes and expanded character interactions to enhance the narrative.

The Origins of Croc

Croc's story begins when a mysterious basket washes ashore on Gobbos Island, carrying a tiny baby crocodile inside. The kind-hearted Gobbos, led by King Rufus, take in the orphaned creature and raise him as one of their own. Over time, Croc grows larger and stronger, becoming a beloved part of their community.

The Rise of Baron Dante

Peace on Gobbos Island is shattered when the evil Baron Dante, a sinister sorcerer with an army of Dantinis, invades the land. Seeking to conquer the island, Dante captures the Gobbos and imprisons them in cages scattered across different worlds. King Rufus manages to summon a magical summoning bell, calling for help—but Croc is the only one who answers.

Croc's Quest to Save the Gobbos

Determined to rescue his family, Croc sets off on a grand adventure, traveling through four distinct islands—Forest, Ice, Desert, and Castle—each filled with traps, enemies, and platforming challenges. Along the way, he must collect crystals and keys to free the Gobbos, defeat powerful bosses, and uncover secret areas.

The Final Battle with Baron Dante

As Croc nears the final island, he confronts Baron Dante in his menacing castle. After an intense battle, Croc defeats Dante and frees the remaining Gobbos. However, just as the Gobbos celebrate their victory, Dante mysteriously vanishes, hinting that his reign of terror may not be over for good.

A Hero's Legacy

With the Gobbos safe once again, Croc is hailed as their hero. Though he remains uncertain about his past and true origins, he knows that the Gobbos will always be his family. As the sun sets on Gobbos Island, Croc prepares for whatever new adventures the future may bring.

The remaster expands on this story with new cutscenes, additional character interactions, and hidden lore elements, giving players a deeper connection to Croc's journey!

1.4 Characters and Enemies

Croc: Legend of the Gobbos Remaster features a colorful cast of characters, from friendly allies to menacing foes. The remaster enhances their designs and adds more expressive animations while keeping their classic charm.

Main Characters

Croc

The brave and kind-hearted protagonist. Raised by the Gobbos, Croc embarks on a quest to rescue his family from Baron Dante. In the remaster, Croc has smoother animations, expressive facial features, and new abilities for better movement and combat.

King Rufus

The wise and benevolent leader of the Gobbos. He is the one who found Croc as a baby and raised him alongside the other Gobbos. He plays a bigger role in the remaster with expanded dialogue and backstory.

The Gobbos

Small, furry creatures that Croc considers family. They are friendly, playful, and unfortunately, often captured by Baron Dante and his minions. Rescuing them is Croc's main mission.

Beany Bird

A friendly bird who serves as Croc's guide throughout his journey. In the remaster, Beany Bird provides hints and tutorials, helping new players get used to the game's mechanics.

Villains and Enemies

Baron Dante

The main antagonist of the game, Baron Dante is a cruel sorcerer who seeks to rule over Gobbos Island. He commands an army of Dantinis and uses dark magic to imprison the Gobbos. The remaster expands his backstory, making him an even more intimidating villain.

The Dantinis

Baron Dante's mischievous henchmen. These small, reptilian creatures come in different forms, some using weapons while others charge at Croc. Their AI has been improved in the remaster, making them smarter and more unpredictable.

Boss Enemies

Each world features a powerful boss at the end, serving as a major challenge for Croc. Some of the most notable ones include:

- Flibby the Giant Fish 🐟 – A massive piranha-like creature that attacks Croc in the water.
- Chumly the Polar Bear 🐻❄️⬜ – A strong but slow ice boss with a devastating ground pound.
- Flame-Breathing Dragon 🔥⬜ – A ferocious fire dragon guarding the Desert Island.
- Baron Dante's Final Form 🏰 – A more powerful and monstrous version of Baron Dante in the final battle.

2. GAMEPLAY MECHANICS & CONTROLS

2.1 Movement and Camera Controls

The remaster of *Croc: Legend of the Gobbos* improves upon the original movement system, making platforming smoother and more responsive.

Basic Movement

- Croc can move in all directions with improved analog stick support.
- Running speed is now more fluid, allowing better control over jumps and landings.
- Mid-air adjustments enable more precise platforming compared to the original's rigid movement.

Jumping and Platforming

- Croc's jump height and distance are influenced by how long the jump button is held.
- A new double-jump feature has been added in specific areas to help with tougher platforming sections.
- Wall kicks and ledge grabbing have been introduced for better level navigation.

Camera Controls

- The remaster features a fully adjustable camera with manual rotation, reducing issues with blind jumps.
- Players can toggle between different camera modes for a more comfortable experience.
- Auto-focus on key areas ensures that important objects and enemies remain in view.

2.2 Combat Mechanics and Attacks

The combat system has been refined to make Croc's attacks more responsive and effective.

Basic Attacks

- Croc's signature tail swipe now has a wider hitbox, making it easier to hit enemies.
- A ground-pound attack has been added, useful for breaking objects and stunning enemies.
- Jump attacks allow Croc to defeat enemies by stomping on them, similar to classic platformers.

Defensive Maneuvers

- A dodge roll mechanic lets Croc evade incoming attacks.
- Blocking has been introduced in select encounters where enemies use projectiles.

Enemy Interactions

- Different enemy types require different strategies, such as hitting weak spots or avoiding counterattacks.
- Some enemies have more advanced AI, making them react dynamically to Croc's movements.

These improvements ensure that combat feels more engaging while staying true to the original game's design.

2.3 Puzzle-Solving Elements

Croc: Legend of the Gobbos Remaster retains classic puzzle elements while introducing new mechanics to enhance gameplay. Players must solve puzzles to unlock doors, activate platforms, and rescue trapped Gobbos.

Switch and Lever Puzzles

- Some levels feature switches that activate moving platforms, open gates, or disable traps.
- Timed switches require quick movement before they reset.

Block and Crate Puzzles

- Pushable blocks may need to be arranged in a specific order to create paths or reveal hidden areas.
- Some crates contain collectibles, while others may activate hidden mechanics.

Key and Door Challenges

- Special colored keys must be found to unlock cages containing Gobbos.
- Some doors require multiple keys or solving a challenge before they can be accessed.

Environmental Interactions

- Pressure plates may need to be weighed down to keep doors open.
- Certain puzzles involve activating objects in a specific sequence.

These mechanics encourage exploration and problem-solving while ensuring that each level feels interactive and rewarding.

2.4 Health, Lives, and Game Over

Croc: Legend of the Gobbos Remaster refines the health and life system to balance difficulty while making the game more accessible.

Health System

- Croc has a three-heart health system by default, which can be upgraded in later levels.
- Taking damage from enemies or hazards removes one heart.
- Collecting red crystals restores lost health.

Lives and Checkpoints

- The game retains a life system, where collecting enough crystals rewards an extra life.
- Checkpoints are strategically placed in each level, reducing the frustration of restarting long sections.
- In easier difficulty modes, players may have unlimited retries instead of a traditional life counter.

Game Over and Continue System

- If Croc loses all his lives, the player can continue from the last checkpoint or restart the level.
- The remaster introduces auto-saving, preventing progress loss.
- Players can revisit previous levels to collect more lives and improve their performance.

These adjustments ensure a fair challenge while providing modern quality-of-life improvements.

3. COLLECTIBLES AND SECRETS

3.1 Gobbos: Their Importance and Locations

Gobbos are the small, furry creatures that Croc must rescue throughout his adventure. They serve as the heart of the game's objective and are essential for unlocking secret levels and achieving 100% completion.

Why Gobbos Matter

- Rescuing all the Gobbos in each level unlocks special bonus stages.
- Collecting every Gobbo across all worlds is required to access the true final battle and the game's best ending.
- Some Gobbos give hints or rewards when freed.

Where to Find Gobbos

- Each main level contains six Gobbos, often hidden behind puzzles, locked doors, or inside secret areas.
- Some Gobbos are in plain sight, while others require Croc to find keys or complete platforming challenges.
- The final Gobbo in a level is often locked in a cage, requiring a special golden key to free them.

Finding all the Gobbos in a world grants access to an extra hidden level, rewarding players with additional challenges and collectibles.

3.2 Crystals: Colors and Uses

Crystals serve as the game's primary collectible, scattered throughout each level. They provide protection, extra lives, and access to hidden content.

Crystal Types and Their Functions

1. Blue Crystals
   - The most common type, found throughout all levels.
   - Acts as a shield—if Croc has at least one, he won't lose a life when hit.
   - If Croc takes damage without any crystals, he loses a life.
2. Red Crystals
   - Restores one heart of Croc's health.
   - Less common than blue crystals and usually found near difficult platforming sections.
3. Green Crystals
   - Awarded in secret or hard-to-reach areas.
   - Collecting all in a level may unlock a hidden Gobbo or bonus content.
4. Golden Crystals
   - Rare and often hidden in breakable crates or secret rooms.
   - Grant extra lives when collected in high numbers.

Managing crystals is key to survival, as they act as both a defense mechanism and a way to earn extra attempts at tough challenges.

3.3 Secret Levels and Unlockables

Croc: Legend of the Gobbos Remaster introduces new secret levels and unlockables, giving players more content beyond the main adventure.

Secret Levels

- Each world has one hidden bonus level, unlocked by collecting all Gobbos in that world.
- These levels are more challenging than regular stages, featuring trickier platforming, tougher enemies, and unique rewards.
- Completing all secret levels unlocks a special final stage, leading to the true ending.

Unlockable Costumes and Skins

- New to the remaster, players can unlock alternate outfits for Croc by completing challenges or finding hidden collectibles.
- Examples include:
    - Classic Croc: Default outfit.
    - Explorer Croc: Unlocked by finishing all secret levels.
    - Golden Croc: Rewarded for 100% completion.

Bonus Content and Extras

- A Sound Test Mode allows players to listen to the remastered soundtrack.
- A Character Gallery features 3D models of Croc, the Gobbos, and enemies with background lore.
- Time Trial Mode unlocks after beating the game, letting players race against the clock in each level.

3.4 Hidden Easter Eggs

The remaster includes several hidden references and secrets for dedicated players to discover.

References to Other Games

- A hidden island in the background of certain levels resembles the home of Fox McCloud, a nod to Argonaut Games' involvement in early *Star Fox* development.
- A secret cave contains a retro-styled Croc sprite, referencing the game's early development as a *Yoshi* prototype.

Classic Developer Easter Eggs

- Some levels feature hidden Argonaut Games logos as a tribute to the original developers.
- Entering a special code on the title screen unlocks commentary from the developers, explaining game design choices.

Mysterious Hidden Room

- A hard-to-reach area in one level contains a strange, unused enemy model, hinting at cut content or a scrapped boss fight.

These hidden details reward players for exploring thoroughly, adding replay value and nostalgia for long-time fans.

4. WORLD 1: FOREST ISLAND

4.1 Level Breakdown and Walkthrough

Croc: Legend of the Gobbos Remaster consists of multiple levels across four main worlds, each with unique themes, platforming challenges, and enemies. Below is a breakdown of the game's structure and general walkthrough strategies.

World 1: Forest Island

- Overview: A beginner-friendly world with grassy landscapes, wooden bridges, and gentle platforming challenges.
- Key Challenges: Simple enemy encounters, moving platforms, and basic switch puzzles.
- Boss Fight: Flibby the Giant Fish – Avoid water attacks and strike when it jumps.

World 2: Ice Island

- Overview: Slippery terrain, icy caves, and frozen lakes make movement more challenging.
- Key Challenges: Slippery surfaces, falling icicles, and precision platforming.
- Boss Fight: Chumly the Polar Bear – Dodge ground pounds and strike when it roars.

World 3: Desert Island

- Overview: A world filled with sand dunes, pyramids, and scorching heat.
- Key Challenges: Sand traps, quicksand pits, and fire-based enemies.
- Boss Fight: Flame-Breathing Dragon – Avoid fireballs and attack during cooldown phases.

World 4: Castle Island

- Overview: The final and most difficult world, featuring dungeons, moving spikes, and tricky platforming.
- Key Challenges: Timed puzzles, enemy waves, and long levels with fewer checkpoints.
- Final Boss Fight: Baron Dante's True Form – A multi-phase battle requiring strategic movement and attack timing.

Each world also contains hidden levels, unlocked by rescuing all Gobbos in that region.

4.2 Enemy Types and Boss Fight

The remaster introduces smarter AI and refined attack patterns for enemies and bosses.

Common Enemy Types

- Dantinis: Baron Dante's minions come in different forms, some wielding weapons, others charging at Croc.
- Spiked Snails: Slow-moving enemies that require tail attacks to defeat.
- Jumping Scorpions: Found in the desert levels, they leap at Croc when approached.

- Ghostly Knights: Castle Island foes that phase in and out, making them difficult to hit.

Boss Fight Strategies

Each world ends with a unique boss that requires pattern recognition and timing.

- Flibby the Giant Fish (Forest Island): Avoid jumping in the water, attack when it lunges.
- Chumly the Polar Bear (Ice Island): Jump over shockwaves and attack when it stops moving.
- Flame-Breathing Dragon (Desert Island): Stay behind cover when it breathes fire, attack when it pauses.
- Baron Dante's True Form (Castle Island): A multi-phase fight where he summons minions, fires projectiles, and transforms. Players must use all learned mechanics to win.

With careful planning and understanding of attack patterns, players can defeat each boss and progress through Croc's adventure.

4.3 Collectibles and Secrets

Croc: Legend of the Gobbos Remaster is filled with collectibles and hidden secrets that reward exploration. Collecting everything is essential for unlocking bonus levels, extra lives, and the true ending.

Main Collectibles

- Gobbos:

- o Each level contains six Gobbos hidden in different locations.
  - o Some are in plain sight, while others require solving puzzles or using hidden paths.
  - o The last Gobbo in each level is trapped in a cage, requiring a golden key to rescue.
  - o Collecting all Gobbos in a world unlocks a hidden bonus level.
- Crystals:
  - o Blue Crystals act as a shield against damage.
  - o Red Crystals restore lost health.
  - o Golden Crystals grant extra lives when a certain number are collected.
  - o Some levels feature hidden crystal rooms with extra rewards.
- Golden Keys:
  - o These unlock Gobbos cages, usually placed near the end of the level.
  - o Some require players to backtrack or complete a side challenge.
- Secret Teleporters:
  - o Some levels feature hidden teleport pads that transport Croc to bonus areas filled with extra lives, crystals, or missing Gobbos.
- Developer Easter Eggs:
  - o References to Argonaut Games and hidden nods to *Star Fox* and other classic games.
  - o A hidden cave in Castle Island contains unused enemy models from the original game.

4.4 Tips for 100% Completion

Fully completing *Croc: Legend of the Gobbos Remaster* requires patience, exploration, and mastering the game's mechanics. Here are the best strategies to achieve 100% completion:

Rescue All Gobbos

- Carefully search each level for hidden rooms and locked cages.
- Look behind waterfalls, inside breakable walls, and in areas that require tricky jumps.
- If you miss a Gobbo, replay the level and check branching paths.

Master the Platforming

- Practice double jumps, wall kicks, and ledge grabs to reach difficult areas.
- Use camera controls to get a better view of platforms and hidden ledges.
- Take time to learn the movement mechanics to avoid unnecessary falls.

Keep an Eye on Crystals

- Always carry at least one blue crystal to avoid losing a life when hit.
- Break every crate and explore side paths for hidden crystal stashes.
- Collecting a high number of crystals grants extra lives, which are useful in later levels.

Defeat Bosses Efficiently

- Learn their attack patterns and wait for the right moment to strike.
- Use dodge rolls and jumps to avoid damage.
- Keep crystals stocked up to avoid losing a life during the fight.

Find Every Secret Level

- Completing all secret levels is necessary to unlock the true final boss fight.
- Some levels require collecting every Gobbo before the bonus stage unlocks.

Use Save Points and Checkpoints Wisely

- The remaster introduces auto-saving, but manually saving after tough sections prevents progress loss.
- If struggling with a section, revisit older levels to gather extra lives before attempting difficult challenges.

By following these tips, players can experience everything *Croc: Legend of the Gobbos Remaster* has to offer and unlock the best possible ending.

5. WORLD 2: ICE ISLAND

5.1 Level Breakdown and Walkthrough

World 2: Ice Island introduces icy landscapes, frozen lakes, and chilling winds that make platforming and combat more challenging. Players must adapt to slippery surfaces and time their movements carefully to avoid hazards.

Level 1: Frosty Caverns

- A beginner-friendly ice level that introduces slippery terrain and basic ice enemies.
- Key obstacles: ice-covered platforms, slow-moving ice blocks, and Dantini ice archers.
- Hidden Gobbos: One is located inside a secret cave behind a frozen waterfall.

Level 2: Snowy Cliffs

- Features long, narrow platforms with gusting winds that push Croc off balance.
- Key obstacles: icy slopes, breakable ice bridges, and rolling snowballs.
- Hidden Gobbos: Found inside breakable ice pillars and behind moving platforms.

Level 3: Glacier Tunnels

- A cave-based level with underground frozen lakes and moving ice platforms.
- Key obstacles: timed jumps over freezing water, ice-spike traps, and collapsing ledges.
- Hidden Gobbos: One requires backtracking after triggering a switch to open a hidden door.

Level 4: Chumly's Ice Fortress (Boss Level)

- A large ice castle filled with enemy ambushes and slippery platforms.
- Boss: Chumly the Polar Bear
    - Phase 1: Chumly charges toward Croc—players must dodge and counterattack.
    - Phase 2: The floor becomes slippery, requiring careful movement to avoid falling off.
    - Final Hit: Chumly gets dizzy after an attack, creating an opening for Croc to land the final blow.

Each level requires mastering movement on ice to progress efficiently while collecting all Gobbos and avoiding hazards.

5.2 Slippery Terrain Challenges

Slippery surfaces are a core difficulty mechanic in Ice Island, making precise platforming more difficult.

How Slippery Terrain Affects Movement

- Croc takes longer to stop after moving, leading to potential missteps and falls.
- Jumping on ice provides less traction upon landing, requiring players to adjust mid-air.
- Running too fast on slopes may cause Croc to slide uncontrollably.

Strategies for Navigating Slippery Terrain

- Tap the movement stick instead of holding it down to control momentum.

- Jump instead of running to stop faster when approaching a ledge.
- Use walls and obstacles to slow down movement when sliding too fast.
- Time jumps carefully to avoid over-sliding into hazards or off platforms.

Hazards Unique to Ice Levels

- Freezing Water: Falling into icy lakes results in instant damage unless quickly escaped.
- Rolling Snowballs: Some levels feature large snowballs that can push Croc off platforms.
- Breakable Ice Bridges: Walking on these too long causes them to crack and collapse.

Mastering these challenges is essential to progressing through Ice Island and reaching the next world.

5.3 Ice Monster Boss Strategies

The Ice Island boss battle takes place in Chumly's Ice Fortress, where Croc faces Chumly the Polar Bear, a massive, aggressive foe who uses the slippery environment to his advantage.

Chumly the Polar Bear - Boss Battle Breakdown

Phase 1: Ice Charge Attack

- Chumly starts by charging at Croc in a straight line.
- Strategy: Dodge to the side at the last second to make him crash into the walls, stunning him for a brief moment.
- Attack Chumly's exposed belly with a tail whip while he is stunned.

Phase 2: Ice Platform Meltdown

- The battlefield begins to break apart, leaving smaller, icy platforms.
- Chumly now jumps between platforms, creating shockwaves on impact.
- Strategy: Jump to another platform before Chumly lands to avoid falling off or taking damage.
- Hit him when he takes a second to recover from a failed jump.

Final Phase: Snowstorm Frenzy

- Chumly summons an icy blizzard, making visibility lower and movement even slipperier.
- He now attacks by launching giant snowballs that roll across the arena.
- Strategy: Use well-timed jumps to dodge snowballs and wait for Chumly to get tired.
- Land the final hit after dodging three snowball waves.

Quick Tips for Beating Chumly

- Keep moving to avoid his charge attacks.
- Jump instead of running to regain control on slippery platforms.
- Attack only when he is stunned—rushing attacks can lead to getting knocked off the arena.

Once defeated, Chumly falls through the ice, and Croc receives a special key that unlocks the next world: Desert Island.

5.4 Collectibles and Secret Paths

Ice Island is filled with hidden areas, teleporters, and secret paths that lead to valuable collectibles.

Hidden Gobbo Locations

- Level 1 (Frosty Caverns): One Gobbo is hidden behind a frozen waterfall—players must break the ice with a stomp attack.
- Level 2 (Snowy Cliffs): A Gobbo is found inside a snowman, requiring Croc to tail whip it.
- Level 3 (Glacier Tunnels): A secret room with Gobbos can only be accessed by activating a hidden switch behind ice pillars.
- Boss Level (Chumly's Ice Fortress): A Gobbo is locked behind a golden door, which requires a special key found in a previous level.

Crystal Stashes and Extra Lives

- Crystals are hidden in snow piles that must be stomped to reveal.
- A hidden teleporter in Glacier Tunnels leads to an area filled with golden crystals and an extra life.
- Secret pathways behind ice walls often contain bonus crystals and keys.

How to Find Secret Levels

- Collecting all Gobbos in Ice Island unlocks a hidden ice-themed bonus level.
- The teleporter cave in Level 3 leads to a bonus challenge with extra lives and rare collectibles.

By mastering Ice Island's platforming, uncovering secret paths, and defeating Chumly, players will be fully prepared for the challenges awaiting in Desert Island.

6. WORLD 3: DESERT ISLAND

6.1 Level Breakdown and Walkthrough

World 3: Desert Island introduces scorching landscapes, ancient ruins, and dangerous quicksand pits. This world requires precise platforming and careful movement to avoid heat-based hazards.

Level 1: Sandy Dunes

- A beginner-friendly stage introducing quicksand, rolling tumbleweeds, and basic fire-based enemies.
- Key Obstacles: Sinking sand, jumping scorpions, and fire geysers.
- Hidden Gobbo: Inside a breakable sandstone wall near the end of the level.

Level 2: Pyramid Ruins

- A maze-like level filled with moving platforms, spike traps, and locked doors.
- Key Obstacles: Timed puzzles, hidden levers, and falling stone blocks.
- Hidden Gobbo: Found inside a secret chamber accessed by pushing a hidden switch.

Level 3: Blazing Canyon

- A high-speed platforming level featuring narrow paths and constant environmental dangers.
- Key Obstacles: Crumbling bridges, rolling boulders, and lava pits.
- Hidden Gobbo: Requires using a hidden teleport pad to access a secret ledge.

Level 4: Fire Temple (Boss Level)

- A lava-filled dungeon with rising heat waves and fire-spewing statues.
- Boss: Flame-Breathing Dragon
  - Uses fire breath attacks and summons flaming Dantinis to fight.
  - Strategy: Hide behind pillars to avoid fire blasts, then attack when the boss pauses.

After defeating the boss, Croc earns a golden key to unlock the next world: Castle Island.

6.2 Avoiding Traps and Quick Sand

Desert Island is full of environmental hazards that can slow progress or lead to instant failure.

Quick Sand Mechanics

- Croc sinks slowly if standing still but can escape by rapidly jumping.

- Some quicksand pits have hidden platforms that lead to secret areas.
- Avoid deep quicksand—these are instant-fail areas with no escape.

Common Desert Traps

- Rolling Boulders: Timed movements are required to avoid getting crushed.
- Fire Geysers: Sprout flames at intervals—observe their pattern before crossing.
- Spike Pits: Appear randomly in the sand, requiring quick reflexes to jump over.

Best Strategies to Survive Traps

- Move constantly in areas with sinking sand to avoid getting stuck.
- Watch for shadows above to predict rolling boulders.
- Use ledge grabs to recover from near-falls into hazards.

6.3 Defeating the Fire-Based Boss

The Flame-Breathing Dragon is one of the toughest bosses, using intense fire attacks and quick movements.

Phase 1: Fire Breath Waves

- The dragon shoots three waves of fire, forcing Croc to dodge.
- Strategy: Hide behind stone pillars until the fire attack stops.

Phase 2: Lava Pool Summon

- The dragon raises lava levels, making certain platforms disappear.
- Strategy: Stay on the remaining safe platforms and prepare for a jumping attack opportunity.

Phase 3: Flaming Dantini Minions

- The dragon summons fire-armored Dantinis that chase Croc.
- Strategy: Defeat the minions first, then attack the dragon's weak point (its open mouth).

Final Hit Opportunity

- After three successful attacks, the dragon becomes stunned, allowing one final tail whip to finish the battle.

6.4 Hidden Gobbos and Collectibles

Desert Island contains some of the hardest-to-find collectibles, requiring players to explore carefully.

Hidden Gobbo Locations

- Level 1: Behind a breakable wall near the quicksand pits.
- Level 2: Inside a hidden pyramid chamber—players must push a secret block to reveal the entrance.
- Level 3: Found on a hidden ledge accessed by a teleporter.
- Boss Level: Hidden behind a lava waterfall, requiring a precise jump to access.

Other Collectibles

- Golden Crystals: Found inside fire statues—players must use tail whips to break them.
- Extra Lives: A secret teleporter in Pyramid Ruins leads to an area filled with extra lives.

By mastering the traps, collecting all Gobbos, and defeating the Fire Dragon, players can advance to the final world: Castle Island.

7. WORLD 4: CASTLE ISLAND

7.1 Level Breakdown and Walkthrough

World 4: Castle Island is the most challenging world in *Croc: Legend of the Gobbos Remaster*, featuring treacherous platforming, powerful enemies, and dark, eerie castle corridors. Players will need to master movement and combat mechanics to survive.

Level 1: Haunted Hallways

- Introduces eerie castle corridors filled with moving platforms, swinging axes, and ghostly enemies.
- Key Obstacles: Timed trap doors, spiked floors, and shadowy Dantinis that can disappear and reappear.
- Hidden Gobbo: Found behind a hidden bookshelf that slides open when Croc tail-whips a specific switch.

Level 2: Tower of Trials

- A vertical ascent level where Croc must scale a massive tower while avoiding collapsing platforms and cannonball traps.
- Key Obstacles: Rotating spike pillars, moving platforms, and flying enemies that attack mid-jump.
- Hidden Gobbo: Requires a risky jump onto a rotating platform that only appears for a few seconds.

Level 3: Lava Dungeon

- A fiery underground level where Croc must navigate across sinking platforms and avoid Dante's fire minions.
- Key Obstacles: Lava pits, crumbling bridges, and swinging chains that must be used as grappling points.
- Hidden Gobbo: Located in a secret chamber behind a destructible wall.

Level 4: Baron Dante's Castle (Boss Level)

- A massive fortress filled with Dante's strongest minions, leading up to the final boss battle.
- Key Obstacles: Timed escape sequences, disappearing floors, and magic barriers requiring keys to unlock.
- Final Boss: Baron Dante (see 7.3 for details).

After clearing this world, players reach the true ending, provided they have collected all Gobbos throughout the game.

7.2 Stronger Enemies and Platforming Challenges

Castle Island introduces some of the toughest enemies and platforming sections in the game.

Stronger Enemies

- Shadow Dantinis: Can phase in and out of visibility, making them difficult to hit.
- Armored Knights: Require multiple tail whips to defeat and charge at Croc aggressively.
- Fire Wraiths: Hovering ghost-like enemies that shoot fireballs from a distance.
- Lava Golems: Large, slow-moving creatures that cause shockwaves when they stomp the ground.

Advanced Platforming Challenges

- Rotating Platforms: Require perfect timing, as they spin rapidly and can drop Croc if not jumped off in time.
- Moving Chain Swings: Some areas require Croc to grab chains and swing across dangerous gaps.
- Vanishing Floors: Certain floors disappear when stepped on, forcing players to move quickly.

Survival Tips

- Use camera adjustments to plan jumps carefully before moving.
- Take advantage of enemy attack cooldowns to find openings for counterattacks.

- Time jumps at the peak of platform movements to avoid missing ledges.

7.3 Baron Dante's Minions & Boss Fight Prep

Before facing Baron Dante, Croc must defeat his Elite Minions, each guarding different parts of the castle.

Miniboss 1: The Dantini Warlord

- A heavily armored Dantini that wields a massive axe.
- Strategy: Wait for him to get stuck after a heavy swing, then attack from behind.

Miniboss 2: The Phantom Sorcerer

- A ghostly figure that summons shadow creatures to attack Croc.
- Strategy: Destroy the summoned shadows first, then attack the sorcerer when he becomes vulnerable.

Miniboss 3: The Lava Beast

- A molten golem that can create fire shockwaves.
- Strategy: Jump over shockwaves and attack when the creature's core is exposed.

Final Boss: Baron Dante
Phase 1: Arena Battle

- Baron Dante fights Croc in an open courtyard, using long-range energy blasts and quick melee strikes.
- Strategy: Dodge his energy waves and counterattack after he misses a punch.

Phase 2: Dark Form Awakens

- Dante transforms into a larger, shadow-powered form with increased speed and damage.
- New Attacks: Shadow projectiles, teleport dashes, and shockwave slams.
- Strategy: Keep moving, avoid telegraphed attacks, and strike when Dante pauses.

Phase 3: The Final Strike

- Dante becomes weaker but enraged, summoning Dantini reinforcements.
- Strategy: Ignore minions and focus all attacks on Dante to finish him off.

Once defeated, Baron Dante is sealed away, and Croc rescues the final Gobbos, unlocking the true ending if all collectibles have been found.

7.4 Final Collectibles and Secrets

Castle Island contains some of the rarest and hardest-to-find collectibles in the game.

Hidden Gobbo Locations

- Haunted Hallways: Behind a hidden bookshelf puzzle.
- Tower of Trials: On a disappearing rotating platform near the top.
- Lava Dungeon: Inside a secret lava chamber, requiring a risky timed jump to access.
- Baron Dante's Castle: Locked inside a golden cage—requires finding a hidden key from an earlier level.

Final Crystals and Extra Lives

- Golden Crystals: Hidden inside armored knight statues that must be tail-whipped to break.
- Extra Lives: Found in secret teleport rooms accessed by activating hard-to-find switches.

Secret Ending Unlock Conditions

- Players must collect all 100 Gobbos across every world.
- Completing the game with all collectibles unlocks a secret bonus stage and an extended epilogue cutscene showing what happens after Croc's victory.

By mastering Castle Island, defeating Baron Dante, and collecting everything, players can truly complete *Croc: Legend of the Gobbos Remaster* at 100%.

8. BOSS FIGHTS AND STRATEGIES

8.1 Understanding Boss Patterns

Each boss in *Croc: Legend of the Gobbos Remaster* follows a distinct attack pattern. Learning these patterns is key to avoiding damage and striking at the right moment. Here's a general breakdown of common boss behaviors:

Common Boss Attack Patterns

1. Charge Attacks – Some bosses rush at Croc in a straight line. Strategy: Sidestep or jump to avoid.
2. Projectile Attacks – Many bosses shoot fireballs, energy blasts, or other projectiles. Strategy: Dodge or use obstacles for cover.
3. Shockwave Attacks – Large bosses create damaging shockwaves when they stomp. Strategy: Jump right before impact.
4. Summoning Minions – Some bosses summon additional enemies. Strategy: Take out weaker minions quickly before refocusing on the boss.
5. Defensive Phases – Certain bosses enter a temporary invulnerable state. Strategy: Wait for their cooldown period to land an attack.

8.2 Best Tactics for Each Boss

Boss 1: Chumly the Polar Bear (Ice Island)

- Weakness: Stuns himself when crashing into walls.
- Tactic: Dodge his charge and hit his exposed belly when he's stunned.
- Advanced Tip: Jump between floating ice platforms to avoid his shockwave attack.

Boss 2: Fire Dragon (Desert Island)

- Weakness: Becomes vulnerable after breathing fire.
- Tactic: Hide behind stone pillars when he breathes fire, then counterattack when he cools down.
- Advanced Tip: Stay on the highest platforms to avoid lava rising during Phase 2.

Boss 3: Phantom Sorcerer (Castle Island Miniboss)

- Weakness: Summoning minions makes him defenseless.
- Tactic: Take out shadow minions first, then attack him when his energy barrier drops.
- Advanced Tip: Time jumps to avoid his homing magic bolts.

Boss 4: Baron Dante (Final Boss)

- Weakness: Long wind-up animations before attacking.
- Tactic: Dodge his energy blasts and wait for an opening after his teleportation attack.
- Advanced Tip: Keep moving at all times to avoid being cornered.

8.3 Avoiding Damage and Attacking Effectively

To defeat bosses efficiently, you'll need to avoid taking unnecessary damage while maximizing your attack opportunities.

Best Defensive Tactics

- Jump Timing: Many attacks, especially shockwaves, can be avoided by jumping at the right time.
- Use Obstacles: Some boss arenas have pillars, rocks, or walls that can be used for cover.
- Movement Control: Stay mobile to avoid getting hit by targeted attacks.

Best Offensive Tactics

- Tail Whip Timing: Most bosses have a brief stun window after attacking—this is the best time to strike.
- Watch for Patterns: Bosses often repeat their attack sequences, so once you identify their rhythm, you can counter more effectively.
- Power-Ups: Some levels contain extra crystals or health pickups before boss fights—use them wisely.

8.4 Final Showdown with Baron Dante

The last fight against Baron Dante is the hardest challenge in the game. The battle takes place in Dante's Throne Room, where he uses dark magic, teleportation, and shockwaves to try and defeat Croc.

Phase 1: Long-Range Attacks

- Dante fires energy blasts in rapid succession.
- Strategy: Dodge side to side and wait for an opening.

Phase 2: Teleportation Strikes

- Dante teleports behind Croc and attempts a powerful melee slam.
- Strategy: Always keep moving and prepare to jump when Dante vanishes.

Phase 3: Summoning Elite Minions

- Dante calls in armored Dantinis to fight Croc while he attacks from a distance.
- Strategy: Defeat the minions first to avoid being overwhelmed.

Final Phase: Dark Energy Overload

- Dante enters an enraged state, creating massive shockwaves and throwing energy orbs.
- Strategy: Jump over shockwaves, dodge energy orbs, and wait for Dante to pause before landing the final hit.

Final Strike

- After three successful counterattacks, Dante weakens.
- Croc lands the finishing tail whip, defeating him for good.

Once Baron Dante is vanquished, Croc rescues the final Gobbos and watches the true ending cutscene if all collectibles have been obtained.

Mastering these boss fights will ensure players complete *Croc: Legend of the Gobbos Remaster* at 100% completion!

9. BONUS CONTENT & REPLAYABILITY

9.1 Unlocking Extra Levels and Features

Croc: Legend of the Gobbos Remaster includes hidden levels, secret features, and bonus content for players who explore thoroughly.

Secret Levels

- Hidden Gobbo Stages – Collect all 6 Gobbos in each main level to unlock bonus challenge levels with harder platforming sections.
- Crystal Caves – Collect all colored crystals in a world to access a hidden crystal cave stage, offering extra rewards.
- Lost Island – The hardest bonus world, unlocked only after 100% completion (all Gobbos, crystals, and secret stages cleared).

Extra Features

- Costume Unlocks – Finding specific hidden collectibles unlocks alternate outfits for Croc.

- Sound Test Mode – Unlocked after completing the game, allowing players to listen to the soundtrack.
- Boss Rush Mode – Beat the game once to unlock a mode where players fight all bosses back-to-back.

9.2 Time Trial and Speedrunning Tips

For players aiming for speedruns or time trial challenges, mastering movement, enemy avoidance, and level shortcuts is key.

Best Speedrun Techniques

- Jump Optimization – Using Croc's longest jump arcs helps cover distances faster than standard walking.
- Camera Control – Adjusting the camera to look ahead prevents unnecessary stops to reorient movement.
- Enemy Boosting – Some enemy knockbacks can be used strategically to gain momentum or reach higher platforms faster.

Shortcuts & Time-Saving Tricks

- Ice Island Skip – Some slopes allow Croc to slide past entire sections.
- Lava Dungeon Route – In certain areas, players can skip crumbling platforms by precise long jumps.
- Boss Quick Defeats – Some bosses can be tricked into self-damage by baiting them into hazards.

Recommended Speedrun Categories

- Any% – Completing the game as fast as possible without collecting everything.

- 100% Completion – Requires all Gobbos, crystals, and secret levels to be cleared.

9.3 Alternative Endings (If Any)

Depending on the player's progress, *Croc: Legend of the Gobbos Remaster* may offer different ending variations:

Standard Ending (Any% Completion)

- If players defeat Baron Dante without collecting all Gobbos, the game ends with a basic victory scene, but some Gobbos remain trapped.

True Ending (100% Completion)

- Players who collect all 100 Gobbos unlock a longer ending where Croc restores peace to the Gobbo Islands and gets a final hidden cutscene revealing a secret about his past.

Secret Bonus Cutscene

- If all time trials are completed with gold rankings, an extra post-credits scene teases a possible sequel or future adventure.

9.4 New Game+ and Post-Game Challenges

After finishing the game, players can access New Game+, featuring:

New Game+ Features

- Harder Enemies – Dantinis and bosses have increased health and faster attack patterns.
- Reduced Checkpoints – Some levels remove mid-level checkpoints, making runs more challenging.
- Alternative Crystal Locations – Some collectibles move to harder-to-reach spots.

Post-Game Challenges

- Platinum Time Trials – A tougher version of time trials with stricter time limits.
- No-Damage Runs – Completing boss fights or entire worlds without taking damage unlocks rare achievements.
- Hidden Developer Easter Eggs – Certain areas in New Game+ reveal extra developer messages and secret areas.

By mastering New Game+ and post-game content, players can experience *Croc: Legend of the Gobbos Remaster* in its most challenging form!

10. TIPS, TRICKS, AND CHEAT CODES

10.1 Essential Tips for Beginners

For new players diving into *Croc: Legend of the Gobbos Remaster*, here are some key tips to get started:

Mastering Movement

- Use the Analog Stick Wisely – Croc's turning can feel slippery, so adjust movement smoothly rather than making sharp turns.
- Jump Timing Matters – Holding the jump button longer gives Croc a higher jump, which is crucial for reaching distant platforms.
- Tail Whip Momentum – The tail whip can help reposition Croc slightly mid-air, useful for adjusting jumps.

Survival Strategies

- Always Collect Crystals – Crystals act as Croc's health buffer. If you have at least one when hit, you won't lose a life.
- Look for Secret Paths – Many ledges, walls, and waterfalls hide hidden areas with extra Gobbos or lives.
- Defeat Enemies Safely – If unsure about an enemy's pattern, observe before attacking. Some require multiple tail whips to defeat.

10.2 Hidden Tricks to Make the Game Easier

Camera Control Hacks

- Use manual camera adjustments to preview tricky jumps before committing.
- Tilting the camera downward helps align precision jumps, especially on small platforms.

Checkpoint Exploits

- Some levels allow backtracking to checkpoints before a tough section, giving you an extra attempt without restarting the level.

Infinite Life Farming

- Some levels feature respawning extra lives—memorize these spots to stock up before tackling harder levels.

Gliding Hack

- In certain areas, jumping while running down a slope can give Croc extra air time, making it easier to clear large gaps.

10.3 Cheat Codes and How to Use Them

Croc: Legend of the Gobbos Remaster includes classic cheat codes for fun and accessibility. To activate them, enter these codes at the main menu or pause screen.

Common Cheat Codes

- Infinite Lives – Unlocks unlimited attempts.
- Unlock All Levels – Allows instant access to any world.
- Big Head Mode – Makes Croc's head comically large.
- Super Jump – Increases Croc's jump height significantly.
- Invincibility Mode – Prevents Croc from taking any damage.

(Exact button sequences for these cheats will depend on the platform.)

How to Use Cheats Wisely

- While cheats make the game easier, using them may disable achievements and 100% completion rewards.
- They are great for practicing tough sections before attempting them without assistance.

10.4 Fun Challenges for Advanced Players

For experienced players looking for extra challenges, try these custom difficulty modes:

Hardcore Mode (No Damage Run)

- Complete the entire game without getting hit once.
- Optional: Do this in New Game+ mode for an even harder experience.

Speedrun Challenge

- Beat the game under a set time limit (e.g., 2 hours for Any%, 4 hours for 100%).
- Avoid unnecessary fights, optimize jumps, and take shortcuts whenever possible.

Crystal-Only Playthrough

- Collect only colored crystals—no Gobbos, no extra lives, just the bare minimum.

No Tail Whip Challenge

- Complete the game without using Croc's tail whip, meaning you must rely solely on platforming and avoiding enemies.

By attempting these challenges, players can push their Croc skills to the limit and enjoy the remaster in exciting new ways!